DATE DUE

2/14 $19

TOP OF THE FOOD CHAIN

BOA CONSTRICTOR

KILLER KING OF THE JUNGLE

LOUISE SPILSBURY

WINDMILL BOOKS
New York

Published in 2014 by Windmill Books, An Imprint of Rosen Publishing
29 East 21st Street, New York, NY 10010

Produced for Windmill by Calcium Creative Ltd
Editor for Calcium Creative Ltd: Sarah Eason
US Editor: Sara Howell
Designers: Paul Myerscough and Keith Williams

Photo credits: Dreamstime: Picstudio 19b, Sannevdberg 24, Kevin
Swope cover, Vacclav 23b; Shutterstock: Fivespots 20, Guentermanaus 12,
Hannamariah 4, Elliotte Rusty Harold 29, Igorsky 8, Eric Isselee 9t, 15b,
Yuttasak Jannarong 9b, Kefiiir 21, Heiko Kiera 11b, Mitchell Kranz 17b, 27,
Kruglov Orda 6, Lightpoet 5, NatalieJean 7, Roy Palmer 13b, Narcis Parfenti
14, Vadim Petrakov 13t, Andy Poole 15t, Pumpza 17t, Dr. Morley Read 10,
16, 18, 25t, 25b, 26, Howard Sandler 1, 28, Audrey Snider-Bell 19t, Pan
Xunbin 22, 23t, Erik Zandboer 11t.

Library of Congress Cataloging-in-Publication Data

Spilsbury, Louise.
  Boa constrictor : killer king of the jungle / by Louise Spilsbury.
      pages cm. — (Top of the food chain)
  Includes index.
  ISBN 978-1-61533-741-5 — ISBN 978-1-61533-799-6 (pbk.) —
  ISBN 978-1-61533-800-9
  1. Boa constrictor--Juvenile literature. 2. Predatory animals—Juvenile
literature. I. Title.
  QL666.O63S66 2014
  597.96'7—dc23
                          2013003369

Manufactured in the United States of America

CPSIA Compliance Information: Batch #BS13WM: For Further Information contact Windmill Books, New York, New York at 1-866-478-0556

CONTENTS

RAIN FOREST RULER

The boa constrictor is the ruler of the **rain forest**! This mighty snake also lives in deserts, grasslands, and fields, but it prefers rain forests. In these hot and damp places there are many plants to hide among and lots of animals to hunt. Boa constrictors slither through the forest floor and up trees, eating almost anything they can catch, from rats and lizards to birds and monkeys.

A food chain shows the living things that eat each other within a **habitat**. Plants are at the bottom of most food chains. They make their own food using energy from the Sun. Some animals eat the leaves, fruits, and seeds of the plants and then **predators**, such as boa constrictors, eat them.

Boa constrictors are large and powerful snakes.

Links in the Food Chain

Boa constrictors are at the top of their rain forest food chains. One boa constrictor food chain begins with trees. Monkeys eat fruit from the trees and then boa constrictors eat the monkeys. An adult boa constrictor has very few predators, which is why it is at the top of the food chain!

MEET THE BOA

Like other snakes, boa constrictors have long, thin bodies and no arms or legs. Their skin is dry and covered by hard scales, which overlap each other like the tiles on a roof. Scales are thick pieces of dead skin that protect the snake's soft body beneath. Snakes are **cold-blooded**. That means they cannot control their own body temperature, so their bodies are usually as hot or cold as their surroundings.

Some snakes kill **prey** by jabbing their fangs into animals to inject them with **venom**, or poison. Boa constrictors use their sharp teeth to catch prey, but they kill it by squeezing it to death. This is called **constriction**.

Boa constrictors have long bodies, no legs, and short tails.

KILLER FACT

Boa constrictors have very flexible backbones that are connected to around 400 ribs. This allows the snake to twist and coil its body so it can get into all sorts of places and catch all sorts of prey!

Boas have flexible bodies and very sharp teeth.

SUPER SNAKES

One reason why boa constrictors are at the top of the food chain and can kill and eat large prey is their size. Most boa constrictors grow up to 13 feet (4 m) long and weigh more than 100 pounds (45 kg). Being big and heavy means the snakes have the strength and weight to bring down large animals. After eating a big animal, boa constrictors do not need to hunt and eat for a number of days.

Boa constrictors roam the rain forest for up to 35 years, and they grow throughout their lives. When they start to get too big for their skin, they just **shed** it. The skin splits over the snake's snout. It then slowly peels back from the rest of the body to reveal a new layer of skin and scales beneath.

People have seen a boa constrictor that was 18 feet (5.5 m) long!

Boas are so big they even eat large, heavy wild pigs.

Links in the Food Chain

Wild pigs are bigger, faster, and more powerful than farm pigs. They have grayish-black, bristly fur and two sharp **tusks** in each jaw, which they use to attack enemies. They usually feed on roots, plants, nuts, and small animals.

Boa constrictors shed their skin in one long piece.

ON THE MOVE

A boa constrictor has no arms or legs but can move quickly across ground, climb trees, and even swim to catch prey! It uses its muscles to push or pull against rough surfaces. As it does so, it folds and unfolds its body, moving in a wavy pattern. It can also travel with its body straight by moving the skin of its belly forward and then pulling itself along, a little like an earthworm.

To climb trees, a boa bunches up its body in horizontal loops, moves its head forward, and then straightens out its body again. To swim, it curves and turns its body from left to right, making "S" shapes again and again. Each time the snake turns, it pushes the water behind it to push itself forward.

When they are young, boas often climb trees. As they get older and heavier, they hunt on the ground more.

Boas are flexible enough to wind and loop their bodies into all sorts of positions!

KILLER FACT

A boa can grasp and hold things with its tail. The snake climbs trees by wrapping its tail around a branch or trunk for support.

Boas prefer to stay on land, but they can swim well when they need to!

CAMOUFLAGED

The colors and patterns on the boa constrictor's back help it to catch prey. Most boa constrictors are colored brown, cream, or gray and have oval, diamond, or circular patterns across their backs. This **camouflage** helps the snakes blend into the background so animals cannot see them!

Boa constrictors have different colors and patterns depending on the habitat in which they live. Although boa constrictors do not often go into water, when they do their coloring and pattern help to camouflage them in the brown-green waters of rivers and lakes. This helps them to sneak up on unsuspecting prey animals such as capybaras, that feed at the water's edge.

The boa's camouflage makes it hard to see among the rain forest leaves.

12

The capybara eats grasses at the edge of rivers, lakes, and flooded grasslands.

Links in the Food Chain

At over 3 feet (1 m) long and weighing as much as a man, the capybara is the world's largest **rodent**. It has partly-webbed feet for swimming and its eyes and ears are high on its head so it can stay above water.

Some boas are brown to match their habitat.

DARK DESTROYER

Boa constrictors mainly hunt in the fading light at dusk or dawn and in the darkness of night. They don't have ears on the outside of their bodies, so they do not hear sounds in the same way as people. However, they can **sense** when prey is moving nearby by "feeling" the vibrations the animal's movements make in the ground. The snake's jaw bones also sense sound vibrations in the air.

Boa constrictors see well at night because they have straight, upright **pupils** that can get bigger in dim light. This lets in as much light as possible to help the snake see prey that come out at night, such as ocelots.

Boa constrictors hunt alone, slithering along and looking out for any signs of prey.

Boas see and sense when ocelots are nearby at night.

Links in the Food Chain

The ocelot is twice as big as a pet cat. It has good eyesight and hearing and hunts rabbits, rodents, iguanas, and frogs at night. It can climb trees to catch monkeys and birds and also swims to catch fish.

A boa's pupils are designed to let in as much light as possible to help the animal spot prey.

SUPER SENSES

The boa constrictor uses a very smart trick to make sure it finds all possible prey. It uses its tongue to "smell" other animals. As it moves through the darkness, it sticks out its forked tongue to pick up scents and tastes in the air. This guides the snake to its next meal.

When the boa pulls its tongue back into its mouth, it passes the scents and tastes it has picked up onto a patch on the roof of its mouth called the Jacobson **organ**. This organ then passes messages to the brain, which figures out what the scents and tastes are. The boa then knows what type of prey is there and how to find it.

The boa constrictor flicks its tongue in and out all the time when it is hunting.

KILLER FACT

Boa constrictors also have small pits on the front of their faces that act as heat sensors. The pits sense heat given off by a nearby animal's body to help the snake figure out what and where it is.

Reptiles smell using the tip of their tongue. A forked tongue with two tips helps them to figure out which direction a smell is coming from.

17

SNEAKY HUNTERS

Boa constrictors are big, heavy snakes, so they cannot move as quickly as many of their prey. Instead they use their camouflage to sneak up on prey or they lie in wait for prey to pass by. Sometimes a boa finds an animal burrow and waits by the entrance for the animal to come out. Boa constrictors also lurk by water, waiting for animals to come to drink.

These smart predators also lie in wait at cave openings and in trees to catch birds and bats that fly past. They wrap their tail around a branch to hold on to it. Then they swing out the rest of their body to catch animals that fly past in their hungry jaws!

Boas remain still and hidden until prey comes close. Then they strike!

This boa is patiently waiting to catch prey that may fly past it.

Boas grab bats in the air as the bats fly by, searching for food.

Links in the Food Chain

Bats are the only **mammals** in the world that can fly. They rest during the day in caves or trees and fly out at night to catch insects or to feed on ripe fruits.

ATTACK!

A boa constrictor is patient while it waits, but when prey passes by it attacks with deadly speed and aim. It darts forward quickly, opening its mouth wide as it closes in. Before the animal realizes what is happening, the boa digs its sharp teeth into its body.

Next, the boa quickly wraps its flexible, muscular body around and around its prey. It tightens the coils and squeezes and squeezes. It doesn't do this to crush the prey's bones, but to stop the animal from breathing. As soon as the prey **suffocates** and its heartbeat stops, the boa relaxes its deadly coils.

Boa constrictors use their teeth to catch large and small prey.

Boas do not need to constrict small prey. They just swallow it whole!

KILLER FACT

The boa constrictor has small, sharp teeth that curve backward. Once dug into prey, the teeth act like hooks and stop the prey from wriggling out of the snake's mouth. If the teeth become damaged and fall out, new ones grow in their place.

DINNERTIME

As soon as a boa constrictor has caught and killed its prey, it starts to eat it. Boa constrictors have stretchy **ligaments** that connect the bones in their jaws. This allows the snakes to open their mouths very wide, which is why they can swallow animals that are bigger than they are.

Boas like to eat their prey head first. As they slowly swallow it, muscles inside their body squeeze the prey down through the throat and into the stomach. In the stomach the animal is broken down and digested by strong acids. After a large meal, the snake may not need to eat again for several weeks!

Muscles in the boa's throat squeeze hard to pull the prey down into its stomach.

A boa's jaws unhinge so it can open its mouth wide and swallow prey whole and head first!

KILLER FACT

How does a boa constrictor breathe when its mouth is filled by a large animal that it is slowly swallowing? A special tube in the bottom of its mouth remains open on one side so the snake can take in air.

Boas eat such large prey they can rest for weeks between meals!

BORN TO KILL

Most snakes lay eggs from which their young later hatch. However, female boa constrictors **incubate** eggs inside their bodies and give birth to up to 60 live baby snakes at a time. The babies are 2 feet (0.6 m) long and fully developed.

Female boa constrictors leave their young right after giving birth, so boa constrictors start to live alone within minutes of being born. They slither off into the undergrowth to hide from hawks, wild pigs, and other predators that might try to catch them while they are small. The baby snakes are not helpless, though. They are born knowing how to hunt and soon start to catch their food.

Young boa constrictors look like smaller versions of their parents.

Young snakes start to catch small prey, such as mice, soon after they are born.

Links in the Food Chain

Young boa constrictors start life eating smaller prey such as mice and rats. As they get older and bigger, they need more meat to fill them up. They then begin to hunt and kill bigger and bigger prey to feed their growing bodies.

Young boas climb trees more often than adults to find and catch food.

BOA DANGERS

The main dangers boa constrictors face are from people. Their rain forest habitats are being cut down and the land is being cleared for farms, highways, and towns. This leaves the snakes and their prey without a place to live. When farmers live close to boa habitats, they kill the snakes because they eat the farmers' chickens. Some people also kill the snakes out of fear. Although boas cannot eat humans, they can deliver a painful bite.

People also hunt these snakes to sell their skins and meat. In some places boa constrictor body parts are sold and used in medicines. People also catch boas to sell them as pets. Today, though, many of the snakes bought as pets have been bred from captive snakes.

Rain forests are often cleared by cutting and burning the trees and plants.

Some people hunt boa constrictors and sell their skins to make goods such as belts, boots, and purses.

Links in the Food Chain

Rats gnaw through wood, plastic, and cardboard to steal food. Their dirty paws and droppings contaminate stored food and they carry fleas that spread disease. Boa constrictors are such great rat hunters that in parts of South America people keep the snakes to catch rats.

NO MORE BOAS?

If there were no boa constrictors at the top of a food chain, the whole **ecosystem** would change. Every living thing in the rain forest depends upon one another for survival. If one animal is removed, every other animal and plant is affected. Predators help to maintain the balance of plants and animals within a habitat.

Boa constrictors eat rats and opossums, and help to keep their numbers down. Without boas, the number of rats and opossums would very quickly grow. If there were many more of these animals, they would become pests in some areas. That is why we need boa constrictors to stay at the top of the food chain.

It is important that boas remain at the top of their food chain for the health of other animals and people, too.

Opossums like to eat garbage and can spread disease.

Links in the Food Chain

Opossums are **nocturnal** animals that eat many different types of food, including nuts, fruits, and small animals such as mice, birds, insects, worms, and snakes. They are also **scavengers** that eat dead animals and waste food that many other animals will not.

GLOSSARY

camouflage (KA-muh-flahj)
When an animal has colors or patterns
that help it blend in with its background.

cold-blooded (KOHLD-bluh-did)
Having a body temperature that
increases or drops depending
on the temperature of the
surrounding environment.

constriction (kun-STRIK-shun)
Tightening or squeezing.

ecosystem (EE-koh-sis-tem)
A community of plants and animals
and their physical surroundings.

habitat (HA-buh-tat) The natural
environment in which a living
thing is found.

incubate (IN-kyoo-bayt) To keep
animal eggs warm until they are ready to
hatch.

ligaments (LIH-guh-ments)
Bands of strong tissue that connect
bones together.

mammals (MA-mulz) Animals with
hair on its body that gives birth to live
young and feeds newborns with milk
from its body.

nocturnal (nok-TUR-nul)
Active at night.

organ (AWR-gun) A body part.

predators (PREH-duh-terz) Animals
that hunt other animals for food.

pupils (PYOO-pulz) Black holes
in the center of the eyes that let light
into the eyes.

rain forest (RAYN FOR-est) A thick
forest of tall trees found in very warm,
wet tropical regions.

rodent (ROH-dent) An animal with
gnawing teeth, such as a mouse.

scavengers (SKA-ven-jurz) Animals
that steal food from other animals or
eat food that they find.

sense (SEN-sez) Parts of the body
that detect particular things in the
environment, such as light, chemicals,
and sound waves. The senses give a
living thing information about the
world around it.

shed (SHED) To lose skin or hair.

suffocates (SUH-fuh-kaytz) To die
due to lack of oxygen, because of being
unable to breathe.

tusks (TUSKS) Long, pointed teeth that
stick out of an animal's mouth.

venom (VEH-num) Poisonous fluid
that is released by some animals such as
venomous snakes.

FURTHER READING

Howard, Melanie A. *Boa Constrictors*. Wild About Snakes. Mankato, MN: Capstone Press, 2012.

Lynette, Rachel. *Who Lives in a Wild, Wet Rain Forest?*. Exploring Habitats. New York: PowerKids Press, 2011.

Sexton, Colleen. *Boa Constrictors*. Snakes Alive. Minneapolis, MN: Bellwether Media, 2011.

Simon, Seymour. *Snakes*. New York: HarperCollins, 2007.

Townsend, John. *Amazing Predators*. Animal Superpowers. Chicago, IL: Heinemann-Raintree, 2013.

WEBSITES

For web resources related to the subject of this book, go to: www.windmillbooks.com/weblinks and select this book's title.

INDEX